Collector's Guide to Country Stoneware and Pottery

Don & Carol Raycraft

COLLECTOR BOOKS
A Division of Schroeder Publishing Co., Inc.

The current values in this book should be used only as a guide. They are not intended to set prices, which vary from one section of the country to another. Auction prices as well as dealer prices vary greatly and are affected by condition as well as demand. Neither the Author nor the Publisher assumes responsibility for any losses that might be incurred as a result of consulting this guide.

Additional copies of this book may be ordered from:

COLLECTOR BOOKS
P.O. Box 3009
Paducah, Kentucky 42001
or
Don & Carol Raycraft
RR #8
Normal, Illinois 61761

@ $9.95 Add $1.00 for postage and handling.

ISBN: 0-89145-289-3

Acknowledgements

Kathryn Householter
Datha Doolin
Ellen Tatem
Rose Holtzclaw
Bill Walter
Bob and Judy Farling
Bill Grande
Kip and Linda Jones
Dr. Alex Hood
Bill Schroeder
Steve Quertermous
Joe and Opal Pickens
Stu Miller Salowitz
Lee and Cynthia Sawyer

Photography

Bob Farling
Chris Farling
Carol Raycraft
R. Craig Raycraft
Lee Sawyer

Introduction

If you ever make the effort to study the historical development of American stoneware potteries, give yourself a significant amount of time, some aspirin, and a soft chair.

The initial fact that will emerge is that potteries changed ownership almost as rapidly as the Holiday Inn on the corner changes the sheets. The owner of a pottery was typically a gifted craftsman so absorbed in producing crocks and churns that he had little time for running a business. Kiln explosions, fires, increasing competition, and bankruptcy were an accepted part of daily life.

A potter needed wood for his kiln, clay and a supply of water to make enough stoneware to earn a modest living. The closer he was to a clay deposit, the more likely his business was to stay in operation. If it was necessary to add large transportation costs to the price of his stoneware, the business could not handle the ever increasing competition. Most of the potteries were located on the perimeters of small towns or a few miles out in the country. The ever present potential for fire and the noxious odors given off by the kiln forced pottery owners to locate away from centers of population.

Potteries in New York State, Massachusetts, and southern Vermont generally produced utilitarian stoneware that ranged from butter churns to bed pans. Though utilitarian stoneware was their primary concern, very few eastern potteries made plates, cups or mugs.

Perhaps the first factory outlet stores were established by country potteries that sold their "seconds" and "thirds" to customers at reduced prices. A jug labeled a "second" was still water tight but might have a concave side due to an accident in the kiln.

It is important to keep in perspective that stoneware was inexpensively available in quantity in most areas during the nineteenth century. If a piece was damaged, it was thrown away. Unlike a basket or a piece of woodenware, stoneware could not be simply repaired and used again.

The potteries were often a family operation with the addition of an apprentice and several local women to decorate the stoneware with cobalt slip. Few potteries employed women as "throwers" because of the significant amount of physical labor involved. It took approximately four pounds of clay to make a one gallon jug.

The first stoneware produced in New England potteries had designs scratched into the surface with a sharp wire or nail. The technique, known as sgraffito, was used from the early nineteenth century until the early 1840's. At that point, the growing number of potteries and increased competition forced decorators to find a less laborious and time consuming process.

By the 1870's, stoneware decorators began to be paid by the piece rather than by the day. Decorators could no longer create intricate flowers, birds, animals and scenes on the surface of crocks, jugs and churns. The casual swirl made with a brush dipped in cobalt slip replaced the "chicken pecking corn." The only time a decorator could spend the necessary time was when stoneware was specially ordered as a gift or presentation piece to a retiring employee or a local lodge officer. Prior to the decoration, a price for the piece was negotiated. In the first half of the nineteenth century, a "large" pottery had nine or ten employees. As competition increased, the number of potteries diminished and only a few survived into the twentieth century.

The employees in the country potteries who were not family members often drifted from job to job. It is not unusual to find a particular decorator's unique bird or flower on jugs from different potteries in the same geographical area. The decorators did not think of themselves as artists and rarely, if ever, signed their work.

The stoneware was sold at the pottery or door to door from the back of a wagon. Stoneware was difficult to transport any significant distance because a load was uncommonly heavy and fragile and severly cracked or chipped pieces were impossible to sell.

In 1825, the Erie Canal was completed and rural potteries lost the first of many battles that gradually destroyed the demand for stoneware in the United States.

The canal made it inexpensive for large potteries to transport their products into rural areas that had been previously serviced by loca potteries. The quality of stoneware from pottery to pottery was almost identical and price was the primary factor in making a purchase.

The large potteries eventually broke the task of creating a jug or crock into many simple operations and employed unskilled workers to mass produce stoneware.

In the 1840's glass containers, tableware, and bottles became affordable for the first time. In the late 1850's and early 1860's glass products were actually less expensive than stoneware in most urban areas. The stoneware market continued to lose business as more conveniences came into popular use. Home refrigeration in factory made oak ice boxes altered the manner in which most Americans stored their food in the 1880's. The national prohibition of alcohol sales that went into effect in 1919 destroyed the stoneware whiskey jug and beer bottle business and closed many of the remaining potteries.

Terms

Albany slip-A deep chocolate brown glaze used on stoneware produced in the late nineteenth century and early twenty century. The glaze was commonly used on both the interior and exterior of stoneware pottery. The brown clay was originally discovered and used by potteries in the area around Albany, New York.

Bristol glaze-On late stoneware the creamy white Bristol glaze was often combined with Albany slip to produce a jug with a brown bottom and light upper portion. Bristol glaze was developed in the English community that bares its name. It was commonly used in many American potteries by 1885. Bristol was one of the first glazes that was produced commercially and could be purchased rather than made from a local recipe. It became increasingly popular and dominated the market by the end of World War I.

Craze-A crack or break in the glaze on a piece of pottery.

Earthenware-Earthenware pottery was fired at some point between 1000° and 1200° centrigrade. Stoneware is generally fired at 1200° to 1300°. Earthenware does not fuse or vitrify and is permeable to liquids. It was essential that redware (earthenware) jugs, crocks and bowls be glazed to secure the contents from gradually "bleeding" through. In the early nineteenth century earthenware clays were much more available than clay used for producing stoneware. The glaze commonly used to seal earthenware contained a high concentration of lead. When the earthenware jug or crock was used for storing pickles, sauerkraut, cider, vinegar, or other highly acidic foods, small pieces of the glaze flaked off and dissolved into the contents. The poisoning that often resulted from eating foods stored in the lead glazed earthenware gradually robbed people of their senses and eventually their lives.

Glaze-Stoneware pottery did not need a glaze because it was impermeable to water. A glaze or seal was often added to make the piece easier to clean. The four primary glazes used by American potteries in the nineteenth century were Albany slip, Bristol, alkaline, and salt. The alkaline glaze was used primarily in the South and southeastern United States. It was also called "tobacco spit". The glaze was made by combining wood ashes or lime soaked in water with sand or ground glass. The salt glaze was created by throwing household salt into the kiln at the height of the firing process. The vapor that was produced settled on the exposed surfaces of all the pieces of stoneware stacked in the kiln.

Incised-Pottery was often decorated to make it more appealing to the eye of a potential customer. There were four major techniques used to add the decoration. They included incising, slip cupping (trailing), brush painting and stenciling. Incising involved scratching a flower, bird or patriotic scene into the surface of a piece of pottery before it was fired with a sharpened nail or a piece of wire. Little incising was done after the 1840's due to the lengthy amount of time involved. The incising process is sometimes referred to as sgraffito or scraffito.

Marked-A piece of pottery that is "marked" carries the name of the pottery in which it was made stamped into some portion of it. The potter's mark was used to distinguish one pottery and its location from others. The mark often was made with printer's type and was impressed or stamped into the clay. A "capacity" mark that indicates whether the jug is a three or four gallon container was also stamped or impressed into the clay.

Ovoid-The first pottery crocks, jugs, and churns made in colonial America were pear shaped or "ovoid". An ovoid jug was broad in the shoulders and tapered to a smaller base. The ovoid form can be used to serve as a general dating technique for stoneware. After the 1830's potters gradually began to produce wares with increasingly cylindrical sides. This was done because pottery with cylindrical sides could be made more quickly, stacked more efficiently in the kiln, and was less fragile to transport.

Slip-cupping-A decorating technique also called slip-trailing that leaves a raised line or "trail" of cobalt slip on the surface of the pottery. The decorator used stoneware cup filled with slip to draw his designs in much the same manner as a baker decorating a cake.

Stoneware-Stoneware was fired at higher temperatures than earthenware and is water tight without any glaze. It was easier to clean and less fragile than earthenware and completely safe for food storage. Stoneware crocks, jugs, and jars also did not hold odors like earthenware because the contents could not "soak" into the individual pieces and remain indefinitely.

Yellow ware-Yellow ware was made in huge quantities from the early 1850's until the mid-1920's. It was produced from yellow clays than can be described as finer than earthenware and lighter in weight than the clay used in the making of stoneware. The yellow clay often had its color brightened by the addition of a lead or alkaline glaze. The molded utilitarian yellow ware was made in New Jersey, Pennsylvania, Kentucky and Ohio. The production of potteries in the East Liverpool, Ohio, area was greater than anywhere else in the nation. Most of the American yellow ware consisted of pitchers, jars, chamber pots, food molds, plates, and cups. It is rare today to find miniature pitchers, decorated batter bowls, or canning jars. It is difficult to distinguish yellow ware made in England from similar examples produced in the United States. It is estimated that less than 10% of the yellow ware was "marked". This makes it extremely difficult to document the country or pottery in which a piece was made.

Burger & Co. impressed pottery mark, Rochester, New York, ca. mid-1870's. The single sweep of a stiff brush dipped in cobalt highlighted the pottery's name.

Impressed maker's mark and capacity mark. M.A. Staudinger was one of several owners of the Albany Stoneware Factory in the mid-nineteenth century.

Dramatic slip-trailed sunflower in deep cobalt on two gallon water cooler.

Brush painted apple on stoneware preserve jar.

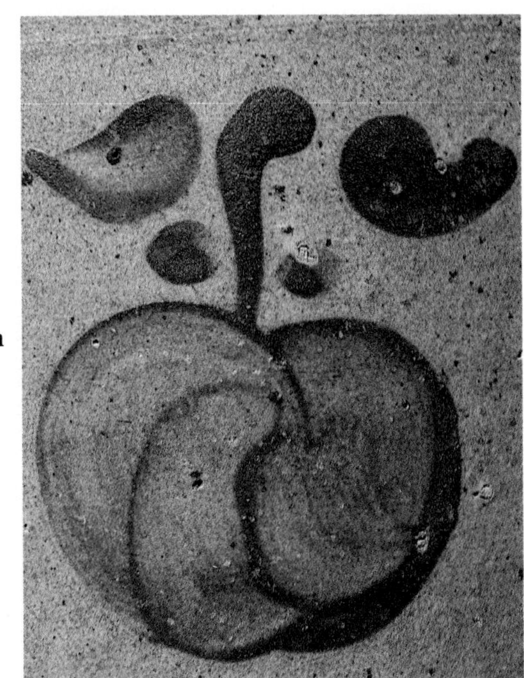

Slip-trailed pecking chicken on two gallon crock.

Ottman Bros. jar with cobalt floral spray. Several New York State potteries adapted the Bennington floral spray to their individual needs.

Incised decoration of a fish on pitcher with no maker's mark.

Slip-trailed standing bird on a branch.

Cobalt flowers and stem with slip-trailed outline and brush painting decoration.

Molded stoneware pitcher, Macomb (Ill.) Stoneware Factory, ca. 1890's.

The jug had to be cut off the potter's wheel with a piece of wire after it had been thrown. If the wire was pulled between the base of the jug and the wheel it left a smooth path.

If the wire was twisted and pulled through, it left a trail of transverse grooves on the bottom of the piece. Oval grooves resembling a finger print remain if a loop shaped wire was used.

Notes on Collecting Stoneware

Decoration

1. Dated pieces of stoneware are rare.
2. Churns, milk pans and batter pitchers seldom are found with elaborate decoration.
3. Many decorators used bits and pieces of several birds to create their own unique birds on the stoneware they decorated.
4. Animals, flags, eagles, sailing ships, fish, human figures or faces, and buildings are rarely found and command premium prices.
5. Simple birds have become uncommon and difficult to find but presently can't be labeled rare.
6. It is interesting that crocks with the "chicken pecking corn" decoration invariably have the chicken pecking to the left and few carry a potter's mark. This decoration is discovered even more rarely on churns and jugs.
7. Midwestern and southern stoneware seldom is found with elaborate decoration because the potteries in these areas came in existence after competition forced stoneware to be produced and sold as inexpensively as possible.
8. Many of the decorators were women who were skillful with slip cup or stiff brush. Several authorities believe that the majority of the incised work was done by men.

Dating a Piece of Stoneware

1. Prior to 1750 little stoneware was made in colonial America.
2. The stoneware that was made in the eighteenth and early nineteenth century was typically incised with simple decorations of fish, flowers or birds.
3. In the early 1800's, the chocolate brown Albany slip was first used to coat the interiors of crocks and jugs. In the early 1900's, Albany slip was commonly used to cover the exterior of crocks and jugs.
4. Slip cupping or trailing became popular in the 1850's and 1860's.
5. After 1870 competition among potteries gradually forced the potter to create stoneware as quickly as possible at the lowest possible price. The amount of decorated stoneware decreased accordingly in the 1880's.
6. The most elaborately brush decorated examples of salt glazed stoneware were created in the period between 1860 and 1880.
7. A great deal of stenciled stoneware was produced in West Virginia and western Pennsylvania from the late 1860's through the early 1900's. The Hamilton and Jones Pottery of Greensboro, Pennsylvania,

was especially active during the later portion of the nineteenth century. Some of the Greensboro pieces had stenciling combined with brush painting.

8. Ovoid (pear shaped) jugs with broad shoulders tapering to a slender base generally predate 1850. The change in form began in the mid-1840's and continued until the sides were completely cylindrical by 1900. The gradual change was necessitated by production demands that could no longer tolerate stacking problems in the kiln and unusual amounts of breakage during transportation to the market place.

Odds and Ends

1. Most potteries made lids for crocks, churns or jars separately to a predetermined size rather than one at a time to match a specific piece of stoneware.
2. Unusual pieces of stoneware fashioned into gate posts, grave stones, bird houses or planters appear so infrequently on the market, it's difficult to establish realistic prices for them.
3. Bennington, Vermont and Albany, Fort Edward, Troy, Lyons and Athens, New York are familiar names to stoneware collectors because of their proximity to the Hudson River or a location along the Erie Canal. This provided great mobility for their wares in a number of geographical areas in the nineteenth century.
4. A skilled and experienced potter could produce between 60 and 90 two to three gallon jugs during a typical work day. The pay prior to the middle of the nineteenth century averaged about $.75 to $1.00 a day with room and board included in the benefit package.
5. In many potteries, balls of clay were prepared and weighed in advance to speed up the throwing process. This allowed the potter who was making three gallon jugs the freedom to grab a ball of clay and be assured of the proper amount of clay to create his piece.
6. There were twelve different marks used for pottery made in Bennington, Vermont, during the nineteenth century. These ranged from the Bennington Factory mark (pre-1823) to Edw'd Norton Co. (1886-1894). The most commonly found Bennington stoneware carries the E. and L.P. Norton mark that was in use between 1861 and 1881. This is by far the longest period of time when a single mark was utilized.
7. Some marks on jugs indicate the firms or businesses the piece was made for and not the pottery in which it was produced. Druggists, grocers, liquor distributors, and mineral water producers often had their name impressed into the jug rather than the pottery.

Jugs

J. and E. Norton one gallon jug, 1850-1859, unusually detailed blue bird on a stump, Bennington, Vermont. The J. and E. Norton period created the most spectacularly decorated examples in the history of the Bennington potteries.

Poland Spring Mineral Water five gallon jug, no maker's mark, quickly executed cobalt blue bird, ca. 1880.

Many New York State and New England potteries made crocks and jugs for liquor distributors, grocers or druggists and put the business name rather than the pottery mark on the piece. This particular mark was impressed into the soft clay along with an especially well defined capacity mark. Printer's type was typically used to make the marks.

Two gallon Thompson and Tyler jug with cobalt flower, ca. 1858-1859.

Thompson and Tyler one gallon jug with an unusual cobalt bird on a branch, ca. 1858-1859, Troy, New York.

Impressed Thompson and Tyler, Troy, New York pottery mark. This is an unusual mark because Thompson and Tyler were in operation for only a short period of time. Most stoneware collectors buy "decoration" rather than a particular pottery mark. An uncommon pottery mark combined with an unusual cobalt decoration is the best of both worlds. Many potteries opened in the eastern United States but were forced to close during the nineteenth century. John Ramsey's *American Potters and Pottery* (1939) attempted to provide a listing of approximate dates of operation. It is almost an impossible task due to sketchy town records and the many changes in ownership at a single pottery. The Bennington, Vermont stoneware potteries went through at least twelve changes in less than a century. The longest single period without change was twenty years (1861-1881).

Edmonds & Co. two gallon jug with cobalt grapes and leaves done with a slip cup. Edmonds & Company was located in Boston, Massachusetts, and operated between 1850 and 1865.

Earthenware three gallon jug, ovoid, ca. 1830-1840's, no maker's mark, splash of cobalt decoration and leaf.

The "3" capacity mark was incised or scratched into the jug rather than impressed with a block of printer's type.

One gallon jug, brush decorated flower and leaf, no maker's mark, ovoid or pear-shaped form. ca. 1830-early 1840's, probably New England.

Two gallon jug, marked "Penn Yan", brush painted flower, ca. 1860's.

Two gallon ovoid jug, marked "J Bennage 1837", impressed with lower case printer's type, splash of cobalt across the mark. It is uncommon to find a dated piece of stoneware. Dated pieces usually have a hastily brushed year but rarely is the date impressed into the jug along with the maker's mark.

Two gallon jug, deep cobalt flower, ca. mid-nineteenth century.

Semi-ovoid three gallon jug, brush decorated flower and leaf, ca. late 1840's-early 1850's.

Unmarked six gallon jug with double handles, brush decoration, ca. 1860's-1870's. The purpose of the second strap handle on this jug was to allow it to be safely picked up. The weight of the jug filled with liquid would present problems and hernias for most thirsty citizens.

Stenciled two gallon jug, not marked with pottery's name, ca. 1880-1900. This example could best be described as a "vendor's" jug because it was specifically made for a wholesale druggist in Detroit, Michigan.

Two gallon ovoid jug, brushed "2" capacity mark, ca. 1830's.

A.P. Donaghho, Parkersburg, West Virginia, three gallon jug, stenciled decoration, late 1870's-early 1880's.

Two gallon jug, redware, no maker's mark, uncommonly found green glaze, ovoid form, ca. 1830. The green color was provided by mixing slip with the scrapings from oxidized copper.

Earthenware jug, Galena (Illinois) Pottery, ca. 1850-1880.

C. Crolius, Manufacturer, New York, brush decorated, impressed maker's mark, uncommon size, ca. 1840's.

Two gallon jug, brush decoration, probably Greensboro, Pennsylvania in origin, ca. 1870's-1880's. The mouth of this jug is almost identical to those found on Hamilton and Jones products of the late nineteenth century. The cobalt "wave" is typical of the Greensboro potteries.

Premium jug, 5½″ high, Albany slip with incised "compliments of" message from W.G. Ginder, Altoona, Pennsylvania, no maker's mark, ca. 1900.

Alkaline glazed three gallon jug with double strap handles, no maker's mark, southern United States, ca. 1860's-1880. Salt was difficult to find in many areas of the South in the 1860's and potters were forced to find a substitute glaze for their wares. A combination of clay, sand and wood ash provided an easily obtainable alternative. The glaze was used in potteries from Texas to Georgia.

E. & L.P. Norton, Bennington, Vermont, molasses pitcher jug, 1861-1881, Albany slip glaze, impressed capacity mark.

C. G. Taylor & Co., Petersburg, Virginia, stenciled maker's mark, ca. 1870's-early 1880's.

Two gallon jug, New York Stoneware Co., Fort Edward, New York, ca. 1870's, floral decoration.

Crocks

Four gallon crock, slip-trailed blue bird, Ottman Bros., Fort Edward, New York, ca. 1870's.

J. and E. Norton, Bennington, Vermont, 1½ gallon crock, slip-trailed cobalt floral design, 1850-1859.

"Chicken pecking corn" two gallon crock, J. Norton & Co., Bennington Vermont, ca. 1859-1861. This slip-trailed chicken is typical of many that can only peck to their right.

Haxstun, Ottman & Co., Fort Edward, New York, four gallon crock, "chicken pecking corn", ca. 1867-1872.

Five gallon crock with cobalt slip-trailed floral decoration, unmarked but probably New York State, ca. late 1870's-early 1880's.

J. & E. Norton, Bennington, Vermont, four gallon crock with great cobalt basket of flowers, 1850-1859. This is a classic example of the quality of workmanship that went into the decoration of a piece of stoneware at Bennington during this period. In later years when competition forced decorators to give up the slip-cup and turn to hastily drawn leafs or swirls, it probably would have been impossible to even specially order such an ornately executed piece.

E. & L.P. Norton, Bennington, Vermont, one gallon crock with simple cobalt decorated leaf, 1861-1881. This same leaf or flower was still being used when the pottery was owned by E. Norton and Co. from 1883-1894.

John Burger, Rochester, New York, five gallon crock with spectacular cobalt cornucopia of flowers and leaves, ca. 1855-1866.

J. and E. Norton, Bennington, Vermont, five gallon crock with elaborate cobalt leaf and floral spray design, 1850-1859.

Five gallon crock with three large cobalt leaves, John Burger, Rochester, New York, ca. 1855-1866. Compare the capacity mark "5" on this crock with the capacity mark "5" on the Burger cornucopia. There is no question that the same decorator worked on both pieces.

John Burger two gallon crock with cobalt lily and leaf decoration, ca. 1855-1866.

Burger & Co., Rochester, New York, four gallon crock with cobalt daisy and leaf, rare mark, ca. 1876.

F.B. Norton and Co., Worcester, Massachusetts. four gallon crock, cobalt parrot and branch, ca. late 1870's. The E. Norton and Co. (1883-1894) of Bennington made almost an identical parrot that faced left rather than right. Frank B. Norton was a grandson of John Norton (died 1828), the founder of the first pottery in Bennington.

J.A. & C.W. Underwood, Fort Edward, New York, one gallon crock with cobalt bird on a branch design, rare mark, ca. 1865-1867.

F.T. Wright & Son, Taunton, Massachusetts, ca. 1855-1868, one gallon crock with cobalt bird on a branch.

J. Shepard, Jr., Geddes, New York, six gallon crock with extensive cobalt floral decoration, ca. 1857-1864. Five and six gallon crocks are not as commonly found as three or four gallon crocks. The weight of a six gallon crock filled with pickles or potatoes would almost necessitate a horse drawn wagon to move it from room to room.

W. Hart, Ogdensburgh, New York, four gallon crock, slip-trailed duck, ca. 1870's-early 1880's.

Six gallon "partridge in a pear tree" crock, no maker's mark, slip-trailed decoration, probably New York State, ca. 1870's.

Six gallon crock, no maker's mark, impressed "6" capacity mark, probably made in the midwest, brush decorated cobalt flower, ca. late nineteenth century.

Elverson and Sherwood, New Brighton, Pennyslvania, ca. 1880-1900, two gallon crock, stenciled decoration. The stenciled crock has little appeal to collectors of decorated stoneware. It was created in the dying days of the American stoneware industry and decorated by running a brush across a stencil pressed against the side of the crock. There is little deviation from crock to crock and minimal chance for human error or self expression.

Peoria Pottery three gallon crock, Peoria, Illinois, ca. 1880. This crock was molded rather than thrown by hand on a potter's wheel.

Contemporary crock from the Beaumont Pottery, York, Maine, ca. 1983. In recent years there have been problems in some areas when nineteenth century salt glazed stoneware with a maker's mark and *no* decoration is recycled to some extent and a cobalt bird or flower is added. Contemporary potter Jerry Beaumont incises the date and his mark into the bottom of each of his pieces so there can never be a question about age. This crock with a teddy bear can make a point if you pay close attention. Be wary of an ovoid jug with a brush painted bird or floral scene. The age of the jug does not match up with the decoration. Teddy bears came before the American public initially about 1903. A Teddy bear on a piece of stoneware from the mid-nineteenth century should immediately raise some emotional red flags.

Contemporary crock from the Beaumont Pottery, ca. 1983. An old jug or crock that was marked with the pottery's name and not decorated is relatively simple to find. The problem arises when the nineteenth century stoneware has its "decoration enchanced" or completed in the 1980's. The Beaumont Pottery creates the finest reproduction stoneware of the twentieth century. There is a significant difference between a reproduction and a "fake". A reproduction is created to provide a collector with a realistically priced alternative to an old example. The workmanship and decoration may be of the same quality as the original, but the reproduction is almost always signed or dated to avoid any confusion. The purpose of the "fake" is to deceive. The collector often pays a premium price because of the quality and condition of the piece. Many times the private collector or dealer who sells the "fake" has also been fooled. It is a wise move to always request a receipt when a purchase is made that describes and dates the piece in addition to the selling price.

E. & L.P. Norton, Bennington, Vermont, three gallon crock, cobalt floral decoration.

Six gallon crock, probably midwestern, no maker's mark, brush painted flower and capacity mark, ca. 1870's-early 1880's.

N.A. White & Son, Utica, New York, ca. 1850's, slip-trailed flower and leaf, one gallon crock.

E. & L.P. Norton, Bennington, Vermont, one gallon crock, 1861-1881, deep cobalt leaf.

A. Conrad, New Geneva, Pennsylvania, three gallon crock, stenciled decoration, ca. 1888's.

Unmarked two gallon crock, brush painted flower and capacity mark, ca. 1870's.

Three gallon crock, slip-trailed capacity mark and swirl, probably midwestern, ca. 1880.

R. Mugler, Buffalo, New York, three gallon crock, deep cobalt floral decoration, ca. 1860.

Slip-trailed blue bird, unmarked three gallon crock, probably New York State, ca. 1870's.

Stenciled butter or cake crock, ca. 1880's, made in Pennsylvania by F.H. Cowden of Harrisburg.

Brush decorated, umarked butter or cake crock, missing a lid, Pennsylvania, ca. 1850-1860, brush decorated. Crocks similar in form to this one were used to brandy fruit cakes. The cake was placed in the crock and a generous order of brandy was poured over it. The lid was placed on the crock and the cake was allowed to dry gradually.

Brush decorated cake crock, Pennsylvania, ca. 1850-1860. Rarely were cake crocks marked with the pottery name or a capacity mark. They can be found in a variety of sizes ranging from six to fourteen inches in diameter.

Pennsylvania cake crock, unmarked, 12″ in diameter, cobalt decoration done with a brush, possibly with a lid from the same pottery. The lids were not made to fit a precise crock. They were created independently and later matched to a crock. It is for that reason that the color of the clay used in the crock and the clay in the lid may not be a perfect match.

Cake or butter crock, 8″ diameter, Pennsylvania, unmarked, ca. mid-nineteenth century, brush decorated.

Macomb, Illinois, three gallon crock, molded, ca. 1900, Bristol glaze, stenciled maker's mark and capacity mark.

Monmouth, Illinois, three gallon crock, molded, ca. 1900, Bristol glaze, stenciled maker's mark and capacity mark.

Two gallon crock, no maker's mark, probably New York State, ca. 1870's, impressed capacity mark.

Ottman Bros., Ft Edward, New York, three gallon crock, slip-trailed standing bird, impressed capacity mark, 1870's.

Deep cobalt bird on a branch, ca. 1860-1870, Cornwall, Ontario, uncommonly wide and thick rim or lip.

N.A. White & Son, Utica, New York, ca. 1870's, uncommonly strong cobalt orchid design, done with a slip-cup and thick glaze.

Whites Utica, deep cobalt orchid, done with a slip-cup and thick glaze, ca. 1870's, impressed capacity mark.

Three gallon crock Burger, Rochester, New York, ca. 1860's, deep cobalt slip-trailed wreath.

Three gallon crock, Lyons Cooperative Pottery Company, Lyons, New York, brushed capacity mark and deep cobalt ''dragon fly'' decoration, ca. 1870's.

Four gallon crock with cobalt floral decoration, ca. 1870's.

Unmarked two gallon crock, slip-trailed capacity mark, ca. 1880.

Specialty Pieces

Brush decorated stoneware pitcher, no potter's or capacity mark, probably Pennsylvania, ca. 1850's.

Heavily decorated pitcher, buff colored stoneware, Pennsylvania, no maker's mark, ca. mid-nineteenth century. Stoneware pitchers were used for storing and dispensing milk, water or beer. Very few are found with a maker's mark.

New York State stoneware pitcher, simple cobalt floral decoration, ca. 1860-1870, no maker's mark.

Stoneware pitcher with deep cobalt tree, no maker's mark, probably New York State, ca. 1850. The front of the pitcher is not glazed due to a stacking problem in the kiln.

White's Utica (New York), three gallon butter churn with cobalt bird on a flower stem, ca. 1865-1877.

Ovoid butter churn, no maker's mark, brush painted flowers, ca. 1840's-early 1850's.

Four gallon butter churn, no maker's mark, thick flower and stem, ca. 1850.

E. Norton & Co. Bennington, Vermont, five gallon butter churn with elaborately executed cobalt floral spray, 1883-1894.

E. Norton & Co. butter churn, floral spray, 1883-1894, impressed capacity mark.

Unmarked "tobacco spit" pitcher, found in North Carolina, ca. late nineteenth century.

"Face" or "grotesque" jug made by Georgia potter Lanier Meaders, twentieth century.

F. H. Cowden, Harrisburg, Pennsylvania, one gallon batter jug, ca. 1887-1895.

The brushed decoration under the pouring spout is combined with a stenciled snowflake design on the back. The tin cover appears to be original but spout cover is missing.

Unmarked batter jug, brushed decoration around spout and drop handles, probably Pennsylvania, ca. 1840's-early 1850's.

Cobalt decorated spittoon, unmarked, 12″ in diameter. The earliest spittons were made of earthenware in a variety of sizes ranging from six inches to fifteen inches. Due to their fragile nature and being constantly underfoot, relatively few have survived.

Stoneware spittoon, 7″ diameter, probably Pennsylvania, ca. mid-nineteenth century, cobalt brushed decoration. The larger "professional" spittoons were designed for court houses and taverns. This size was used primarily in the home.

Four gallon stoneware water cooler, no maker's mark, brushed cobalt decoration, ca. 1860's-1870's, possibly midwestern in origin.

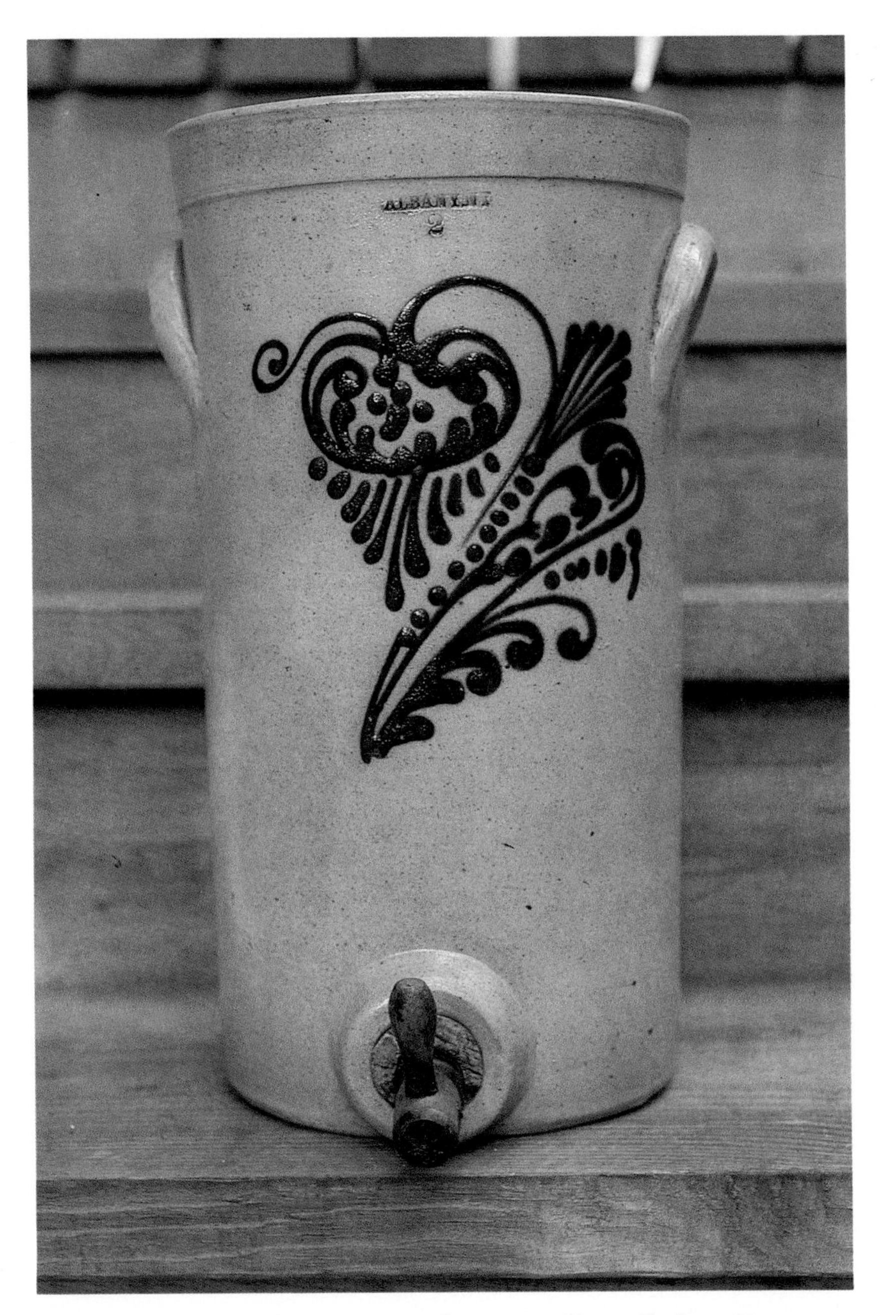

Albany N.Y., two gallon water cooler, great slip-trailed sunflower, ca. 1870-1890.

Heavily decorated water cooler, no maker's mark, probably German in origin, ca. late nineteenth-early twentieth century.

Chicken watering pot, no maker's mark, probably Pennsylvania, made in two pieces and bonded together with slip, ca. 1850-1875.

This type of pot may also be described as a "poultry fountain". The later mass produced versions consisted of a bottomless jug with a small opening being placed in a molded stoneware saucer. These late examples were usually covered with a Bristol white glaze and were made well into the twentieth century. This early "hooded" poultry fountain is of a type rarely found today.

Unusual stoneware measure from country store, no maker's mark, probably made in Kentucky, ca. late nineteenth century.

Jars

J. Norton Co. Bennington, Vermont, two gallon jar, decorated with slip-trailed cobalt floral spray, 1859-1861.

Stoneware jar, no maker's mark, probably New York State, ca. 1880, hastily executed bird decoration.

This jar is unusual because it is also decorated with a cobalt leaf on the reverse side.

C.W. Braun, Buffalo, New York, slip-trailed bird, ca. 1860's, no capacity mark.

J. Norton and Co., Bennington, Vermont, deep cobalt blue bird, "1½" gallon impressed capacity mark, 1859-1861. During the J. Norton period of ownership, jars were produced in seven sizes ranging from four gallon covered jars with the lids resting on the rims to quart size preserve jars with inset covers. The "bird" jar illustrated here has an inset rim.

Five gallon stoneware jar, Hamilton and Jones, Greensboro, Pennsylvania, ca. 1870's-early 1880's, stenciled decoration and maker's mark with brushed swirl.

"Maccoboy" snuff jar, no maker's mark, stenciled decoration, probably West Virginia or Pennsylvania, ca. 1880's.

One gallon storage jar, no maker's mark, probably Pennsylvania or West Virginia, unusual brush painted apple decoration, ca. 1870's-1880's.

Storage jar, ovoid form, splash of cobalt over the maker's mark, Goodwin & Webster, Hartford, Connecticut, ca. 1830's.

Maker's mark impressed with upper case printer's type.

Burger and Lang, three gallon jar with cobalt tulip and leaf design, Rochester, New York, ca. 1870's.

Beaumont Pottery, York, Maine, adaptation of J. and E. Norton 1850-1859 deer, pine tree and fence design on contemporary stoneware jar.

N. Clark, Athens, New York, impressed maker's mark, ca. 1820's-early 1830's, cobalt wreath decoration.

Sixteen gallon storage jar, cobalt floral decoration covering entire front, ca. 1860's, brushed capacity mark. Large storage jars are usually underpriced because most collectors do not have a use or adequate storage space for them.

Three gallon jar, impressed capacity mark, slip-trailed cobalt decoration, dated "1860". It is unusual to find a dated piece. With its semi-ovoid form, it is surprising that this piece was made as late as 1860.

Brush decorated storage jar, flower and leaf decoration, Pennsylvania, ca. 1870's.

Unusual three gallon storage jar, Albany slip with ochre brushed decoration, probably Pennsylvania, ca. 1870's-early 1880's.

Earthenware storage jar, Galena, Illinois, ca. 1850-1880.

Earthenware preserve jar, Galena, Illinois, ca. 1850-1880, salmon colored body with mottled green glaze.

Two gallon storage jar, inset lid, brush decorated flower and capacity mark, impressed "Lyons", made at the Lyons (New York) Pottery, ca. 1850's.

Four gallon brush decorated jar, no maker's mark, impressed capacity mark, ca. 1860's.

Storage jar, brush decorated, four gallon, probably from the Hamilton and Jones Pottery at Greensboro, Pennsylvania, ca. 1870's-early 1880's.

Twelve gallon storage jar, brush decorated, stenciled maker's mark, ca. 1880.

Williams and Reppert, Greensboro, Pennyslvania, eight gallon storage jar, combination of brush and stenciled decoration, ca. 1870's-early 1880's.

Stenciled preserve jar, buff colored clay, probably Pennsylvania or West Virginia in origin, ca. 1870's, no maker's mark.

Preserve jars, unmarked, brush decoration, probably Greensboro, Pennsylvania area, ca. 1880.

James Hamilton, Greensboro, Pennsylvania, jar stenciled and brush decorated, ca. 1870's-early 1880's.

Stenciled James Hamilton & Co. jar with "2" capacity mark, Greensboro, Pennsylvania, ca. 1870's. The Hamilton Pottery in Greensboro was also known as the Eagle Pottery.

James Hamilton "3" jar, Greensboro, Pennsylvania, ca. 1870's, steciled decoration with brush stroke around rim. The upper portion of this jar is warped to the point that it was probably sold at the pottery as a "second."

James Hamilton preserve jar, Greensboro, Pennsylvania, ca. 1870's, stenciled "fan" decoration and brush work around rim and base.

Preserve jar, no maker's mark, buff colored clay, simple brushed cobalt decoration, ca. 1880's.

Demuth's Snuff, Lancaster, Pennsylvania, vendor's jar, ca. 1890's, no maker's mark.

Neff Brother's "2" Manufacturers, Taylorsville, Ohio, ca. 1900, no maker's mark.

J. Hamilton jar, Greensboro, Pennsylvania, stenciled decoration, ca. 1870's.

Bayless McCarthey & Co., Louisville, Kentucky, stenciled and brush decorated preserve jar, ca. 1880.

Two gallon jar, cobalt decoration, impressed capacity mark, probably New York State, ca. 1870's.

Covered stoneware jar, ovoid form, brushed cobalt capacity mark, no maker's mark, inset lid, ca. mid-nineteenth century, probably New York State.

Goodwin and Webster, Hartford, Connecticut, jar, brushed decoration around handles and across impressed maker's mark, ca. 1830's.

Two gallon jar, stenciled capacity and maker's mark, E.S. & B, new Brighton, Pennsylvania ca. late nineteenth century.

Donaghho Co., Parkersburg, W. Virginia stenciled crocks and a canning jar with an inset lid, late nineteenth century.

Redware jars, made in Pennsylvania, no maker's mark or decoration, ca. mid- nineteenth century.

Greensboro, Pennsylvania stoneware jars, stenciled decoration, ca. 1880's.

Redware

Pie plate, earthenware, 7″ diameter, slip-trailed "waves", Pennsylvania, ca. 1840's-1860's.

Pie plate, earthenware, 6″ diameter, slip decorated, ca. 1840's-1860's.

Earthenware pie plates, not decorated, probably made in eastern Pennsylvania, ca. 1840-1860's, no maker's mark. Pie plates were glazed only on the inside. The exterior of plate was left unglazed and should be black with carbon. The plates were formed around a mold in such a way that the baked pie could be slpped from the plate onto a serving dish. The pies were never cut in the earthenware plate because the knife could easily break the glazed interior.

Earthenware pie plates, eastern Pennsylvania, ca. 1840's-1860's. The plate at right was simply decorated with a slip-cup. Some examples had words or short phrases written in slip.

Contemporary earthenware pie plate with extensive slip decoration.

Redware apple butter crock with strap handle, no maker's mark, Pennsylvania in origin, ca. 1850-1870, unglazed exterior and glazed interior. This apple butter crock would have been used on the dinner table and passed from person to person.

Earthenware pot, probably for flowers, found in central Illinois, no maker's mark, ca. late nineteenth century. This could be described as an "end of the day" piece or a "whimsey" that was quickly crafted by a potter in the closing minutes of his work day as a gift.

Redware milk pan, no maker's mark, probably Pennsylvania in origin, ca. 1850, glazed interior, 7½″ diameter.

Earthenware storage jar, no maker's mark, probably Pennsylvania, ca. mid-nineteenth century.

Yellow Ware

In recent years there has been a significant increase in demand for the yellow ware pottery that was produced for household use from the 1850's through the 1920's.

The majority of the American-made yellow ware was manufactured in Ohio, Pennsylvania, and New Jersey. Seldom was a maker's mark used because many companies were producing almost identical wares.

The most commonly found pieces of yellow ware today are mixing bowls, plates, pitchers, molds and cups. The more difficult pieces to acquire include tobacco jars, soap holders, spittoons and small pitchers.

Yellow ware was molded rather than hand thrown in England, Canada, and the United States. The handles on pitchers, cups, mugs and chamber pots were applied by hand. As few pieces are "signed", it is extremely hard to differentiate among American, English, and Canadian yellow ware.

Stoneware mug with cobalt bands, yellow ware mug with cobalt bands, unmarked, ca. late nineteenth century.

Mugs with white slip bands, no maker's mark, ca. late nineteenth century.

Mugs with blue and brown bands, no maker's mark, ca. late nineteenth century.

Cup with "mocha" decoration, ca. mid-nineteenth century, probably made in England.

Pitcher and mixing bowl, brown bands, ca. late nineteenth-early twentieth century, no maker's mark.

Tobacco jar, early twentieth century, no maker's mark.

Pitcher, white slip bands, early twentieth century, no maker's mark.

Chamber pot, wide white slip band, ca. mid-nineteenth century. Chamber pots could be purchased with or without covers.

Rolling pin, one replaced pine handle, ca. late nineteenth-early twentieth century, no maker's mark.

Yellow ware plates, 8″ diameters, no maker's mark, ca. early twentieth century.

Yellow ware plate, 7″ diameter, no maker's mark ca. early twentieth century.

Soap dish, uncommonly found, no maker's mark, ca. late nineteenth century.

Yellow ware jar, brown and white slip bands, twentieth century, no maker's mark.

Mixing bowls, slip decorated bands, early twentieth century.

Stoneware custard cups with blue slip bands and sponge decorated custard cup, early twentieth century.

Yellow ware bowls, variety of sizes and slip bandings.

Mixing bowls and pitcher illustrating variety of glazing decorations.

Food mold.

Food molds showing variation in glazing of the yellow ware.

Price List

Page 18
J. and E. Norton one gallon jug - $350.00-395.00

Page 19
Poland Spring Mineral Water five gallon jug - $325.00-375.00

Page 20
Thompson and Tyler two gallon jug - $300.00-400.00

Page 21
Thompson and Tyler one gallon jug - $625.00-675.00

Page 22
Edmonds & Co. two gallon jug - $425.00-475.00

Page 23
Earthenware three gallon jug - $250.00-275.00

Page 24
One gallon ovoid jug - $150.00-175.00

Page 25
"Penn Yan" two gallon jug - $125.00-150.00

Page 26
Two gallon ovoid jug - $200.00-240.00

Page 27
Two gallon jug - $115.00-130.00

Page 28
Semi-ovoid three gallon jug - $160.00-200.00

Page 29
Double-handled six gallon jug - $130.00-145.00

Page 30
Stenciled two gallon jug - $80.00-110.00

Page 31
Two gallon ovoid jug - $130.00-145.00

Page 32
A.P. Donaghho three gallon jug - $165.00-185.00

Page 34
Earthenware jug - $200.00-240.00

Page 35
C. Crolius brush decorated jug - $200.00-225.00

Page 36
Two gallon brush decorated jug - $105.00-140.00

Page 37
Premium jug - $85.00-115.00

Page 38
Alkaline glazed three gallon jug - $250.00-285.00

Page 39
Molasses pitcher jug - $125.00-140.00

Page 40
C.G. Taylor & Co. stenciled jug - $75.00-100.00
New York Stoneware Co. two gallon jug - $85.00-110.00

Page 41
Ottman Bros. four gallon crock - $275.00-300.00

Page 42
J. and E. Norton 1½ gallon crock - $350.00-375.00

Page 43
J. Norton & Co. "chicken pecking corn" two gallon crock - $700.00-800.00

Page 44
Haxstun , Ottman & Co. "chicken pecking corn" four gallon crock - $500.00-600.00

Page 45
Cobalt slip-trailed five gallon crock - $200.00-240.00

Page 46
J. & E. Norton four gallon crock - $600.00-750.00

Page 47
E. & L.P. Norton one gallon crock - $140.00-160.00

Page 48
John Burger five gallon crock - $3000.00-3500.00

Page 49
J. & E. Norton five gallon crock - $500.00-575.00

Page 50
John Burger five gallon crock - $850.00-925.00

Page 51
John Burger two gallon crock - $250.00-275.00

Page 52
Burger & Co. four gallon crock - $250.00-300.00

Page 53
F. B. Norton & Co. four gallon crock - $550.00-675.00

Page 54
J. A. & C. W. Underwood one gallon crock - $350.00-385.00

Page 55
F. T. Wright & Son one gallon crock - $335.00-375.00

Page 56
J. Shepard Jr. six gallon crock - $1000.00-1200.00

Page 57
W. Hart four gallon crock - $300.00-375.00

Page 58
Six gallon "partridge in a pear tree" crock - $450.00-550.00

Page 59
Brush decorated six gallon crock - $95.00-120.00

Page 60
Elverson and Sherwood two gallon crock - $85.00-120.00

Page 61
Peoria Pottery three gallon crock - $70.00-85.00

Page 64
E. & L.P. Norton three gallon crock - $125.00-150.00

Page 65
Six gallon brush painted crock - $120.00-145.00

Page 66
N. A. White & Son one gallon crock - $115.00-130.00

Page 67
E. & L.P. Norton one gallon crock - $115.00-130.00

Page 68
A. Conrad three gallon crock - $125.00-140.00

Page 69
Unmarked two gallon crock - $100.00-120.00

Page 70
Slip-trail decorated three gallon crock - $100.00-115.00

Page 71
R. Mugler three gallon crock - $150.00-185.00

Page 72
Slip-trail decorated unmarked three gallon crock - $200.00-225.00

Page 73
Stenciled butter or cake crock - $120.00-140.00

Page 74
Brush decorated unmarked butter or cake crock - $200.00-225.00
Brush decorated cake crock - $200.00-225.00

Page 75
Unmarked Pennsylvania cake crock - $285.00-325.00
Unmarked Pennsylvania cake or butter crock - $275.00-300.00

Page 76
Bristol glaze three gallon crock - $50.00-60.00

Page 77
Bristol glaze three gallon crock - $50.00-60.00

Page 78
Two gallon crock - $250.00-295.00
Ottman Bros. three gallon crock - $275.00-350.00

Page 79
Wide rimmed crock-$250.00-300.00
N. A. White & Son crock - $225.00-250.00

Page 80
Whites Utica crock - $225.00-250.00
Burger three gallon crock - $300.00-325.00

Page 81
Lyons Cooperative Pottery Co. three gallon crock - $125.00-150.00
Cobalt decorated four gallon crock - $90.00-115.00
Unmarked two gallon - $55.00-70.00

Page 82
Brush decorated, stoneware pitcher - $350.00-450.00

Page 83
Heavily decorated Pennsylvania stoneware pitcher - $350.00-450.00

Page 84
New York State stoneware pitcher - $275.00-300.00

Page 85
Cobalt decorated stoneware pitcher - $250.00-300.00

Page 86
Whites Utica three gallon butter churn - $1000.00-1200.00

Page 87
Ovoid butter churn - $350.00-450.00

Page 88
Four gallon butter churn - $375.00-450.00

Page 89
E. Norton & Co. five gallon butter churn - $800.00-1000.00

Page 90
E. Norton & Co. butter churn - $500.00-600.00

Page 91
Unmarked "tobacco spit" pitcher - $325.00-400.00
"Face" jug - $250.00-300.00

Page 92
F. H. Cowden one gallon batter jug- $500.00-575.00

Page 93
Unmarked batter jug - $300.00-375.00

Page 94
Cobalt decorated spittoon - $300.00-340.00

Page 95
Cobalt brush decorated spittoon - $275.00-325.00

Page 96
Four gallon stoneware water cooler - $180.0-210.00

Page 97
Two gallon water cooler - $1000.00-1200.00

Page 98
Heavily decorated water cooler - $200.00-275.00
Chicken watering pot - $240.00-300.00

Page 99
Stoneware measure - $65.00-75.00

Page 100
J. Norton Co. two gallon jar - $200.00-240.00

Page 101
Decorated stoneware jar - $160.00-200.00

Page 102
C. W. Braun slip-trail decorated jar - $300.00-375.00

Page 103
J. Norton & Co. 1½ gallon jar - $300.00-350.00

Page 104
Hamilton and Jones five gallon jar - $275.00-350.00

Page 105
"Maccoboy" snuff jar - $100.00-130.00

Page 106
Brush painted one gallon storage jar - $275.00-325.00

Page 107
Ovoid storage jar - $160.00-185.00

Page 108
Burger and Lang three gallon jar - $250.00-300.00

Page 110
N. Clark cobalt decorated jar - $225.00-260.00

Page 111
Sixteen gallon storage jar - $240.00-295.00

Page 112
Dated three gallon jar - $300.00-325.00

Page 113
Brush decorated storage jar - $150.00-175.00

Page 114
Albany slip three gallon storage jar - $300.00-340.00

Page 115
Earthenware storage jar - $240.00-295.00

Page 116
Earthenware preserve jar - $225.00-275.00

Page 117
Lyons Pottery two gallon storage jar - $160.00-185.00

Page 118
Four gallon brush decorated jar - $100.00-120.00

Page 119
Four gallon brush decorated storage jar - $200.00-225.00

Page 120
Twelve gallon storage jar - $275.00-300.00

Page 121
Williams and Reppert eight gallon storage jar - $300.00-335.00

Page 122
Stenciled preserve jar - $45.00-65.00

Page 123
Unmarked preserve jars - $65.00-75.00 each

Page 124
James Hamilton stenciled jar - $95.00-120.00

Page 125
James Hamilton stenciled "2" jar - $100.00-115.00

Page 126
James Hamilton stenciled "3" jar - $90.00-115.00

Page 127
James Hamilton preserve jar - $85.00-100.00

Page 128
Cobalt brushed preserve jar - $65.00-85.00

Page 129
Demuth's Snuff vendor's jar - $45.00-60.00

Page 130
Neff Brother's "2" jar - $55.00-70.00

Page 131
J. Hamilton stenciled jar - $120.00-140.00

Page 132
Bayless McCarthey & Co. preserve jar - $135.00-155.00

Page 133
Cobalt decorated two gallon jar - $150.00-175.00

Page 134
Ovoid covered stoneware jar - $200.00-250.00

Page 135
Goodwin and Webster jar - $230.00-275.00

Page 136
E. S. & B. two gallon jar - $55.00-65.00
Donaghho Co. crocks: "2" - $65.00-75.00, "4"-$75.00-95.00
Canning jar - $70.00-85.00

Page 137
Pennsylvania redware jars - $55.00-75.00
Pennsylvania stenciled stoneware jars - $90.00-115.00

Page 138
7″ Earthenware pie plate - $200.00-250.00
6″ Earthenware pie plate - $150.00-175.00

Page 139
Undecorated earthenware pie plates - $65.00-80.00; $75.00-85.00
Pennsylvania earthenware pie plates - $65.00-85.00; $175.00-200.00

Page 141
Redware apple butter crock - $90.00-125.00

Page 142
Earthenware pot - $50.00-65.00

Page 143
Redware milk pan - $110.00-135.00
Earthenware storage jar - $120.00-145.00

Page 144
Stoneware mug (Peoria Pottery) - $150.00-200.00; yellow ware mug - $30.00-50.00

Page 145
Mugs - $30.00-50.00 Mugs - $30.00-50.00

Page 146
"Mocha" decorated mug - $250.00-300.00
Pitcher - $50.00-70.00; mixing bowls - $15.00-30.00

Page 147
Tobacco jar - $110.00-150.00

Page 148
Pitcher - $50.00-75.00

Page 149
Chamber pot - $100.00-125.00

Page 150
Rolling pin - $100.00-125.00
Yellow ware plates - $40.00-45.00 each

Page 151
Yellow ware plate - $50.00-60.00
Soap dish - $100.00-115.00

Page 152
Yellow ware jar - $60.00-65.00

Page 153
Mixing bowls - $20.00-40.00
Stoneware custard cups - $20.00-30.00 each

Page 154
Yellow ware bowls - $20.00-80.00
Mixing bowls - $20.00-50.00; pitcher - $50.00-75.00

Page 155
Food mold - $35.00-55.00
Food molds - $35.00-55.00

Two Important Tools For The Astute Antique Dealer, Collector and Investor

Schroeder's Antiques Price Guide

The very best low cost investment that you can make if you are really serious about antiques and collectibles is a good identification and price guide. We publish and highly recommend **Schroeder's Antiques Price Guide.** Our editors and writers are very careful to seek out and report accurate values each year. We do not simply change the values of the items each year but start anew to bring you an entirely new edition. If there are repeats, they are by chance and not by choice. Each huge edition (it weighs 3 pounds!) has over 56,000 descriptions and current values on 608 - 8½x11 pages. There are hundreds and hundreds of categories and even more illustrations. Each topic is introduced by an interesting discussion that is an education in itself. Again, no dealer, collector or investor can afford not to own this book. It is available from your favorite bookseller or antiques dealer at the low price of $9.95. If you are unable to find this price guide in your area, it's available from Collector Books, P. O. Box 3009, Paducah, KY 42001 at $9.95 plus $1.00 for postage and handling.

Flea Market Trader

Bargains are pretty hard to come by these days -- especially in the field of antiques and collectibles, and everyone knows that the most promising sources for those seldom-found under-priced treasures are flea markets. To help you recognize a bargain when you find it, you'll want a copy of the *Flea Market Trader* -- the only price guide on the market that deals exclusively with all types of merchandise you'll be likely to encounter in the marketplace. It contains not only reliable pricing information, but the *Flea Market Trader* will be the first to tune you in to the market's newest collectible interests -- you'll be able to buy before the market becomes established, before prices have a chance to escalate! You'll not only have the satisfaction of being first in the know, but you'll see your investments appreciate dramatically. You'll love the format -- its handy 5½″ x 8½″ size will tuck easily into pocket or purse. Its common sense organization along with a detailed index makes finding your subject a breeze. There's tons of information and hundreds of photos to aid in identification. It's written with first-hand insight and an understanding of market activities. It's reliable, informative, comprehensive; it's a bargain! From Collector Books, P. O. Box 3009, Paducah, KY 42001 at $8.95 plus $1.00 for postage and handling.